SUCCESSFUL AMERICANS

Americans of Central American Heritage

John F. Grabowski

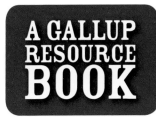

A GALLUP RESOURCE BOOK

Mason Crest Publishers
Philadelphia

Produced by OTTN Publishing in association with
Bow Publications, Inc.

MASON CREST PUBLISHERS INC.
370 Reed Road
Broomall, Pennsylvania 19008
(866) MCP-BOOK (toll free)
www.masoncrest.com

Printed in the United States of America.

First Printing

9 8 7 6 5 4 3 2 1

Library of Congress Cataloging-in-Publication Data

Grabowski, John F.
  Americans of Central American heritage / John F. Grabowski.
    p. cm. — (Successful Americans)
  Includes bibliographical references.
  ISBN 978-1-4222-0525-9 (hardcover)—ISBN 978-1-4222-0859-5 (pbk.)
  1. Central American Americans—Biography—Juvenile literature. 2. Successful
people—United States—Biography—Juvenile literature. I. Title.
  E184.C34G73 2008
  920'.009268'728073—dc22
                                                        2008043952

Publisher's note:
All quotations in this book come from original sources, and contain the spelling
and grammatical inconsistencies of the original text.

◀ **CROSS-CURRENTS** ▶

When you see this logo, turn
to the Cross-Currents section
at the back of the book. The
Cross-Currents features explore
connections between people,
places, events, and ideas.

Table of Contents

CHAPTER 1   Leaving Central America   5

CHAPTER 2   Franklin Chang-Díaz: Astronaut and Scientist   12

CHAPTER 3   Rolando Blackman: Basketball All-Star   17

CHAPTER 4   Carlos Mencia: Comedian   23

CHAPTER 5   Christy Turlington: Supermodel and Entrepreneur   28

CHAPTER 6   Mariano Rivera: Pro Baseball Player   34

CHAPTER 7   Christianne Meneses Jacobs: Magazine Founder   39

CHAPTER 8   America Ferrera: Actress   45

CROSS-CURRENTS   50

NOTES   56

GLOSSARY   58

FURTHER READING   59

INTERNET RESOURCES   59

OTHER SUCCESSFUL AMERICANS OF
    CENTRAL AMERICAN HERITAGE   60

INDEX   62

An immigrant from El Salvador takes part in a rally on immigration reform held in Washington, D.C., in 2006. Many legal immigrants from Central America want the U.S. government to pass legislation allowing illegal immigrants to earn citizenship.

CHAPTER ONE

Leaving Central America

The U.S. Census Bureau estimates that more than 3 million people in the United States are of Central American ancestry. Some are the descendents of emigrants who came from Central America—from Belize, Costa Rica, El Salvador, Guatemala, Honduras, Nicaragua, or Panama. Of the more than 2 million Central America–born immigrants, the majority came from just two countries—El Salvador and Guatemala.

FOREIGN-BORN POPULATION FROM CENTRAL AMERICA

Place of Birth	Number of People Living in the United States
Costa Rica	104,793
Guatemala	874,799
Honduras	490,317
Nicaragua	295,059
Panama	123,631
El Salvador	1,371,666
Other Central American countries	111,825
Total	3,372,090

Source: Place of Birth for the Foreign-born Population; U.S. Census Bureau, 2006 American Community Survey.

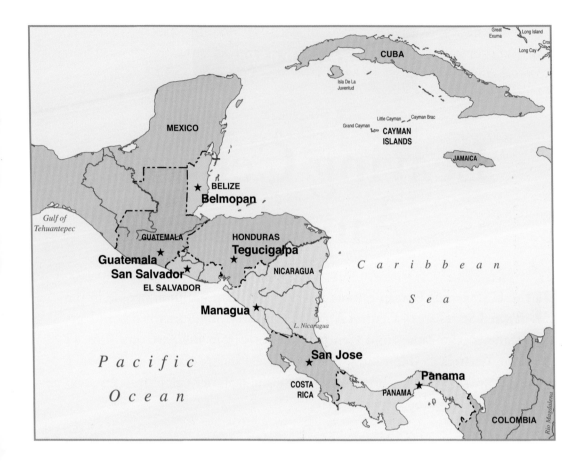

HISTORICAL BACKGROUND

Central America is in the southernmost part of North America. It is a tropical isthmus connecting North and South America that extends from Mexico in the north to Colombia in the south. The region was colonized during the 1500s by Spain as the Kingdom of Guatemala. It included part of today's Mexico, Guatemala, Belize, El Salvador, Honduras, Nicaragua, and Costa Rica.

On September 15, 1821, the region declared independence from Spain and two years later formed the United Provinces of Central America. However, that union was short-lived, breaking up just 15 years later. Although Central America is not politically unified today, many of its countries are members of the

Central American Parliament, a political institution formed in 1991 to promote cooperation among the region's nations. The Central American country of Panama, which once was part of Colombia, is also a member.

The nations of Central American were based on agricultural economies through the 1950s. The majority of the region's inhabitants lived in poverty, with little hope of improving their living conditions. During the 1960s several nations made attempts at building an industrialized economy, but with the exception of Costa Rica, the economy is weak in Central American countries.

INCREASED IMMIGRATION

Before 1970 approximately half of all emigrants from Central American countries relocated to nearby nations. The other half migrated to North or South America. By 1980 that pattern had changed drastically: About 80 percent of emigrants were leaving the region. A decade later, that percentage surged to more than 90 percent.

Of the Central American emigrants who traveled north, some traveled only as far as Mexico. However, increasing numbers came to the United States. According to the 1970 U.S. census, there were around 100,000 emigrants from Central

HISPANIC AMERICANS

Hispanic Americans are U.S. citizens who can trace their roots back to Mexico, Spain, and the Spanish-speaking nations of South America, Central America, and the Caribbean. The U.S. Census Bureau estimates that Hispanics account for 15 percent of the total population in the United States. By the year 2050, that number is expected to increase to 24 percent.

WHO WANTS TO EMIGRATE?

In 2007, the Gallup Organization surveyed residents of countries in Latin America to determine whether they wished to leave their homeland. The responses from Central American countries appear below:

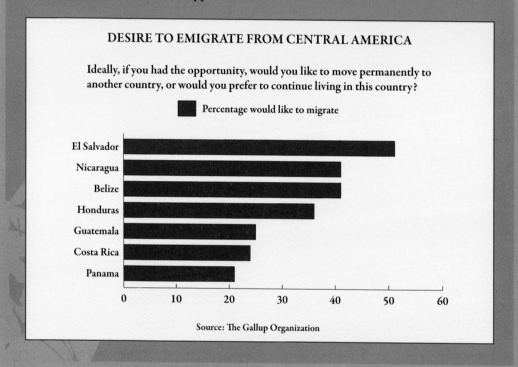

DESIRE TO EMIGRATE FROM CENTRAL AMERICA

Ideally, if you had the opportunity, would you like to move permanently to another country, or would you prefer to continue living in this country?

■ Percentage would like to migrate

Source: The Gallup Organization

America in the United States. By 1980 that number had more than tripled to nearly 350,000. By 1990 it had tripled again to more than a million. In 2000 it passed the 2 million mark.

That number is undoubtedly even higher when taking into account the number of people from Central America who entered the country illegally. According to the Office of Immigration Statistics, there were approximately 720,000 "unauthorized immigrants" from El Salvador and Guatemala alone in 2000, and an estimated 1,040,000 from those two nations in 2007.

FACTORS AFFECTING IMMIGRATION

Since the 1970s poverty, civil unrest, and natural disasters in the Central America region have sparked a rise in immigration to the United States. Thousands have traveled north in hopes of finding safety and a better life for themselves and their families.

Civil wars have caused large-scale emigration from the countries of El Salvador, Guatemala, and Nicaragua. Thousands died in El Salvador from political violence during the1970s and a full-scale war from1980 to 1992. Years of violence shook Nicaragua as the U.S. government supported counter-revolutionary groups fighting against the Sandinista government during the 1980s. In Guatemala a guerrilla war that began in the 1960s and continued until the 1990s caused the deaths of more than 100,000 people and forced more than a million to become refugees.

Natural disasters have also forced many people from their homes. In 1972 an earthquake in Nicaragua killed 10,000 people. Four years later an even more devastating quake in Guatemala was responsible for 23,000 deaths. Central America has also been victimized by powerful hurricanes. Hurricanes Joan (1988), Mitch (1998), Stan (2005), and Felix (2007) have left paths of destruction through Nicaragua, Honduras,

An aerial view of houses destroyed in Krukira, Nicaragua, after being struck by Hurricane Felix in September 2007. Many refugees from hurricanes, floods, earthquakes, and other natural disasters in Central America have come to the United States to start new lives.

◀ **CROSS-CURRENTS** ▶

To learn more about Americans' opinions on overall immigration to the United States, turn to page 50.

and Guatemala. Many of the hundreds of thousands left homeless by earthquakes and storms have traveled north to the United States in an attempt to put their lives back together.

An estimated 374,000 Central Americans are living in the United States under Temporary Protected Status (TPS). TPS is temporary immigration status granted to aliens who cannot return to their homeland safely due to extraordinary temporary conditions, such as natural disasters. The power to assign TPS status for a country originally belonged to the U.S. attorney general, but has since been transferred to the secretary of Homeland Security. As of 2008 El Salvador, Honduras, and Nicaragua were the three Central American nations designated for TPS.

LEARNING ENGLISH

Newcomers from Spanish-speaking countries can have trouble assimilating into U.S. society if they do not know English. According to the U.S. Census Bureau, almost one in five people in the United States speak a language other than English at home. Spanish is the most common language, with more than 28 million people reporting Spanish as the household language. Many Hispanic immigrants believe it is important to learn how to speak English, but they do not want their children to lose their links to their Latin culture.

A 2007 Gallup poll found that the majority of Americans believe that immigrants should be required to demonstrate a high degree of skill in English in order to remain in the United States. A question in the Gallup annual Minority Rights and Relations survey asked if the United States should "require immigrants who come to this country to be proficient in English as a condition for remaining in the U.S." Approximately

77 percent of those questioned answered "yes." Hispanic Americans also supported such a requirement, although with a smaller majority of 59 percent.

FORMING COMMUNITIES

The states with the highest number of foreign-born Central American residents are California, Florida, New York, Texas, and New Jersey. California claims the highest numbers, with more than 700,000. Florida is home to 250,000; New York and Texas each have about 200,000; and New Jersey has around 90,000. Other states with significant Central American immigrant populations are Maryland and Virginia.

Approximately half of all Central American immigrants have settled in five major metropolitan areas. Nearly one out of every four has settled in the area around Los Angeles, California. Four other cities with large numbers of immigrants from Central America are New York; Miami, Florida; Houston, Texas; and San Francisco, California.

There are many U.S. communities in which large numbers of people from specific Central American countries have settled. The town of Sweetwater, near Miami, for example, has the highest percentage of people from Nicaragua. Sweetwater is sometimes called Little Managua, after the capital city of Nicaragua.

The following chapters contain biographies of people who emigrated from Central America or whose parents or grandparents came from a Central American country. These successful Americans have made contributions to the United States in the fields of science, entertainment, and education.

CHAPTER TWO

Franklin Chang-Díaz: Astronaut and Scientist

Born in San José, the capital and largest city of Costa Rica, Franklin Chang-Díaz grew up with dreams of traveling in space. His dreams became a reality after he immigrated to the United States, where he became the first Hispanic American astronaut to travel in outer space. As a physicist and rocket propulsion scientist, Chang-Díaz also served for 12 years as director of the Advanced Space Propulsion Laboratory at the Johnson Space Center, in Houston, Texas.

Franklin Chang-Díaz emigrated from Costa Rica when he was 18 years old to pursue his goal of becoming an astronaut.

A DETERMINED YOUNG MAN

Franklin Chang-Díaz was born in San José on April 5, 1950, to Ramón Chang-Morales, an oil worker of Chinese and Amerindian descent, and María Eugenia Díaz De Chang, who was Costa Rican. He was named in honor of former U.S. president Franklin Delano Roosevelt.

Chang-Díaz has said that one of his earliest memories is of his mother telling him about the Soviet satellite *Sputnik*. Launched on October 4, 1957, by the Union of Soviet Socialist Republics (USSR) it became the first manmade object to orbit the earth. Franklin stayed up for hours that night, sitting in a mango tree hoping to get a glimpse of the satellite as it made its way through the heavens. From that moment on, he says, he knew he wanted to become an astronaut. Together with his cousins, he would play with an old cardboard box, imagining it to be a spaceship taking them to mysterious new worlds. He even wrote a letter to famed German rocket scientist Werner von Braun asking for advice on how to achieve his goal.

To fulfill his dream Franklin decided he would have to go to the United States. After graduating in November 1967 from Colegio de la Salle in San José, he got a job in a bank. He saved his money and soon had enough to travel to Hartford, Connecticut, where he lived with relatives. Although he had completed high school in Costa Rica, he enrolled as a senior at Hartford High School in order to improve his command of English. Despite facing numerous obstacles, he kept at his studies and graduated in 1969 near the top of his class.

The following fall Chang-Díaz enrolled at the University of Connecticut (UConn), in Storrs, where he majored in

COSTA RICA

The nation of Costa Rica lies between Nicaragua and Panama. In area Costa Rica is the fifth-largest country of the seven Central American nations. With just over 4 million inhabitants, it is also fifth largest in population. Rugged mountains, many of which are volcanic in nature, separate its coastal plains. The capital city of San José lies in the Central Valley, in the heart of the country.

Franklin Chang-Díaz: Astronaut and Scientist

mechanical engineering. Under the guidance of one of his professors, Franklin became involved in experimental physics. "What I really wanted to do," he told an interviewer, "was design rockets. I wanted to be like von Braun and rocketry pioneer Robert Goddard."

After graduating from UConn, Chang-Díaz continued his studies at the Massachusetts Institute of Technology (MIT), in Cambridge, Massachusetts. In 1977 he received his doctorate in applied plasma physics. That year he also became a naturalized citizen of the United States. U.S. citizenship is a requirement for becoming an astronaut with the National Aeronautics and Space Administration (NASA) space program.

After making his first flight in 1986, Chang-Díaz would go on to travel on six more missions. In this photo, he was part of the crew onboard Endeavour *as the Space Transportation System (STS) launched from John F. Kennedy Space Center, Florida, in June 2002.*

SETTING RECORDS

After graduation Chang-Díaz took a job in Cambridge working as a fusion physicist at the Charles Stark Draper Laboratory, an applied research and development lab that specializes in space system technology. Before he got his citizenship Chang-Díaz had applied to the astronaut program at NASA but he had been rejected. After he became a U.S. citizen and was working at Draper, he applied a second time. In May 1980 he was accepted as a member of the astronaut corps.

Chang-Díaz finished his astronaut training the following year. Subsequently he helped support various Space Transportation System (STS) missions from the ground. The STS refers to the entire space shuttle system, which includes the components used at launch—a huge, orange external tank and two solid rocket boosters—as well as the orbiter that carries astronauts and mission equipment.

It was not until January 12, 1986, that Chang-Díaz flew on his first space mission. STS 61-C was a satellite deployment and research mission aboard the *Columbia*. The experience of that first flight, he later recalled, was overwhelming:

> I had lots of powerful emotions. When you get to space, as soon as you feel the float, you want to do two things. You want to unstrap because even though you train for zero gravity, you never know exactly what it's like until you're in it. The second thing you want to do is look out the window. That's what blows you away—to see Earth from that point.

Chang-Díaz's next two missions were aboard the orbiter *Atlantis*—the first in October 1989 and the next nearly three years later. In 1994 he took part in the U.S.-Russian Space Shuttle mission aboard the *Discovery*. Franklin made three more flights, in 1996 aboard *Columbia*, in 1998 aboard *Discovery*, and in 2002 aboard *Endeavour*.

During his career as an astronaut Chang-Díaz traveled on a total of seven space flights. He logged over 1,600 hours in space, including more than 19½ hours in three spacewalks. When he made his seventh flight in 2002, he tied the record for most flights. That record was set earlier in the year by NASA astronaut Jerry Ross. Chang-Díaz retired from NASA in 2005 after 25 years of service.

In 2002 Chang-Díaz trains for his seventh and final mission in space, which involved partial assembly of the International Space Station, the research facility that has been orbiting the earth since 1998.

THE SCIENCE OF SPACE EXPLORATION

While performing his duties as an astronaut, Chang-Díaz continued his research in the field of plasma physics. From 1993 to 2005 he was director of the Advanced Space Propulsion Laboratory at the Johnson Space Center in Houston. Upon leaving NASA, he founded the Ad Astra Rocket Company (AARC), a firm that specializes in plasma rocket technology. He is chairman and chief executive officer (CEO) of the company, in which he continues his work in developing advanced rocket engines.

That research has included development of the Variable Specific Impulse Magnetoplasma Rocket (VASIMR), a rocket that uses plasma for propulsion. It provides faster speeds than rocket designs currently used. Chang-Díaz explains, "The objective is to travel to Mars. A propulsion system like the VASIMR would make it possible to get there in a little more than a month, rather than a year. . . . With a propulsion system like this, we'd have the entire solar system within our reach."

Franklin's interests are not limited to rocketry. He is also involved in researching tropical diseases, particularly Chagas disease, which affects from 8 to 11 million people in Mexico, Central America, and South America. He has also performed community service work with chronic mental patients and rehabilitated drug abusers.

◀ **CROSS-CURRENTS** ▶

Despite the great expense of maintaining a space program, NASA has retained the support of the American public, according to Gallup polls. To learn more, turn to page 51.

Chang-Díaz has received many awards and honors for his work. In 1986 he received the Medal of Liberty from President Ronald Reagan at the Statue of Liberty Centennial Celebration in New York City. The medal, which recognized the nation's most distinguished naturalized citizens, was awarded to only 12 recipients. The Congressional Hispanic Caucus awarded Chang-Díaz the Medal of Excellence in 1987.

CHAPTER THREE

Rolando Blackman: Basketball All-Star

Born in Panama City, Panama, Rolando "Ro" Blackman was one of the first players born in Central America to play in the National Basketball Association (NBA). During his 13-year career with the NBA, mostly with the Dallas Mavericks, he was a four-time NBA All-Star and the Dallas Mavericks' all-time leading scorer. Since 2000 he has worked as a player development coach, television analyst, and assistant coach for the Mavericks.

FROM PANAMA TO BROOKLYN

Rolando "Ro" Antonio Blackman was born in Panama City on February 26, 1959. He was named after a Panamanian singer who was a favorite of his

mother, Gloria Blackman. His father, John Blackman, was a computer programmer for the U.S. government. In 1967, when Rolando was eight years old, he and his sister Angela were sent to live with his grandmother in the East

Assistant coach Rolando Blackman talks to Devin Harris of the Dallas Mavericks during a November 2005 game in Dallas, Texas. Blackman was a star player for the Mavs from 1981 to 1992.

Home to more than 3 million people, the country of Panama borders Costa Rica to the northwest and Colombia to the southeast. Panama seceded from Colombia in 1903 and its government signed a treaty with the United States that allowed for the building of the Panama Canal, a waterway that joins the Caribbean Sea and the Pacific Ocean. The country's capital is Panama City.

While playing for the Kansas State University Wildcats in 1980, Blackman was named the Big Eight Conference Player of the Year and All-American.

Flatbush section of Brooklyn, in New York City. His parents followed them north three years later.

As a child, Rolando first took up the sport of soccer, but as he grew older his interests turned to basketball. It took a while for his skills to develop. In junior high school he was cut from his seventh-, eighth-, and ninth-grade teams. But he kept practicing, and eventually made the squad at William E. Grady Vocational High School, in Brooklyn.

In 1977 Blackman graduated from Grady and decided to leave New York for Kansas. He had been accepted at Kansas State University, where he was to play basketball for the Wildcats. Kansas appealed to him, he once explained, "because it was quiet and green and people said hello for no reason. It reminded me of Panama."

ALL-AMERICAN HONORS

Rolando's stay at Kansas State was a memorable one. He ended his collegiate career as one of the best all-around players in school history. His career 1,844 points rank second on the Wildcats' all-time scoring list. He was also named Big Eight Defensive Player of the Year three times. During his senior year Blackman won All-American honors and was cowinner of the 1980–81 Big Eight Athlete of the Year award.

In 1980 Blackman was selected to play on the U.S. men's national basketball team at the Olympics. Unfortunately, the team did not get a chance to compete. That year the Summer Olympic Games were being held in Moscow, in the Soviet Union. After the USSR invaded Afghanistan in December 1979, the U.S. government responded by boycotting the Games.

The following year Blackman experienced one of the most memorable moments of his collegiate career. In March 1981 the Kansas State Wildcats made it to the second round of the National Collegiate Athletic Association (NCAA) Tournament and faced the number-two ranked Oregon State Beavers. The Wildcats battled back from a double-digit deficit and tied the game in the last few minutes of regulation time. With overtime looming, Rolando pulled up for a jump shot just before time expired. Although a Beaver defender hit his arm, the shot still went in to give the Wildcats an upset win. A photograph of Rolando making the winning basket appeared on the March 23, 1981, cover of *Sports Illustrated* magazine.

◀ **CROSS-CURRENTS** ▶

Some people claim that when an athlete appears on the cover of *Sports Illustrated,* bad luck will follow. To learn more about this so-called magazine cover jinx, turn to page 52.

ON TO THE NBA

At the end of the 1981 college basketball season, Blackman entered the NBA draft. The Dallas Mavericks selected him with the ninth overall pick. The fledgling Dallas team had entered the league just a year earlier and finished its first season with the worst record in the NBA, winning just 15 games.

Rolando Blackman: Basketball All-Star

During his eleven years with the Mavericks, Blackman set team records by scoring 16,643 points and 6,487 field goals.

Blackman helped to gradually improve the Dallas team. As a rookie during the 1981–82 season he averaged over 13 points per game and the Mavs won 28 games. The next season he secured a starting spot in the lineup, and raised his average to nearly 18 points per contest as the Mavs had 38 wins. He reached a career-high average of 22.4 points per game in his third year with the team, which recorded 43 wins.

As Blackman continued to improve his game, his team also got better. By the end of the 1986–87 season, the Mavericks had won 55 games and finished on top of the Midwest Division for the first time in the team's history.

A NARROW MISS

Over the years Blackman continued to demonstrate his abilities as a clutch player and deadly shooter. But in the early 1990s the fortunes of the Mavericks began to decline. In 1992 Dallas traded the 33-year-old Blackman to the New York Knicks in exchange for a first-round draft choice.

Rolando made solid contributions to the Knicks during the 1992–93 season, helping New York win an impressive 60 games. After defeating Indiana and Charlotte in the first two rounds of the 1993 NBA playoffs, the Knicks played six games in a hard-fought Eastern Conference finals. However, the New

York team ended its season by losing to the Chicago Bulls, led by superstar Michael Jordan.

Although at the twilight of his career, Blackman took one final shot at a championship. Despite suffering a herniated disk, he played an important role for the Knicks during the 1993–94 season, during which he averaged nearly 15 points a game. The New York team won the Atlantic Division crown, and beat the New Jersey Nets in the first round of the 1994 NBA championship playoffs and the Bulls in the Conference semifinals.

Blackman spent his final two seasons with the New York Knicks, who made it to the NBA playoffs both years.

Rolando Blackman: Basketball All-Star

For the first time in his 13-year NBA career, Rolando was on a team that had reached the finals. The Knicks and the Houston Rockets split the first six games, setting up a decisive Game 7. During that game Rolando sat on the bench as Knicks starting guard John Starks played. New York came up short, losing by a score of 90-84. Years later, coach Pat Riley would say that not replacing Starks with Blackman during that game was the greatest coaching error of his career.

After the championship game Blackman, who was plagued by back problems, retired from the NBA. But he wasn't finished playing. He traveled to Europe, where for the next three years he played for various professional basketball leagues in Greece and Italy before returning to the United States.

OPENING NEW DOORS

Determined to finish his college education, Blackman returned to Kansas State and in 1996 completed his degree in marketing and sociology. "I knew I was intelligent," he explained in an interview, "and it was important for me to get away from the negative stigma that athletes don't complete school."

After receiving his degree, Blackman remained involved with basketball, landing broadcasting jobs with ESPN and CBS. It wasn't long before he was offered a position with the Mavericks as a player development coach, a position he held for five years. In 2006 he was named the team's director of basketball development.

In March 2000 Rolando was honored when the Mavericks retired his number 22 uniform. Kansas State followed suit in February 2007, when the Wildcats retired Blackman's number 25 jersey.

While with the NBA, Blackman participated in charity fundraisers such as the New York All-Star Basketball Classic. Today, he is involved in community service activities such as the Assist Youth Foundation, which helps underprivileged kids in the Dallas/Fort Worth area.

Carlos Mencia: Comedian

The son of a Mexican mother and Honduran father, Carlos Mencia grew up in a Los Angeles barrio. His early success as a stand-up comedian led to several television appearances, and eventually to a popular weekly television show on the cable channel Comedy Central. Mencia's brand of blunt, biting, ethnic humor has earned him many critics but also millions of fans.

TWO FAMILIES

Ned Arnel Mencia was born in San Pedro Sula, Honduras, on October 22, 1967. He was the 17th of 18 children. His mother, Magdelena Mencía, and

father, Roberto Holness, were involved in a domestic dispute at the time of his birth. As a result she listed her family name of Mencia on her son's birth certificate.

The Holness family moved to the United States shortly after

In August 2008 actor and comedian Carlos Mencia accepts an Imagen Award for TV Best Actor. The honor is given by the Imagen Foundation, which annually recognizes positive portrayals of Latinos in the entertainment industry.

The country of Honduras ranks as the second-largest Central American nation in both area and population. Around 7.5 million people live in the country, which is bordered by Guatemala, El Salvador, Nicaragua, and the Caribbean Sea. The capital city is Tegucigalpa. Located in the northwestern part of Honduras is the city of San Pedro Sula, the nation's industrial center, as well as its second-largest city.

Ned's birth. They settled in East Los Angeles, where Ned lived with his aunt and uncle, Consuela and Pablo Mencia. In an interview Ned explained the arrangement:

> My birth father had built our little house behind a bigger house.... But my uncle and aunt lived next door, and they weren't able to have children, so my birth mother gave me away to them, since our own house was so packed. I was the only child in my uncle's house, but I grew up with two moms and two dads, all next door to each other.

As Ned was growing up, he used his father's surname of Holness even though the name Mencia was on his birth certificate. He attended Hammel Grade School in East Los Angeles, but left for a time after he reached his teens. His parents were worried about the influence of gangs in the area, so when he was 12 he went to live for a time in Sico, Honduras. He returned to California a few years later and in 1985 graduated from James A. Garfield High School, in Los Angeles.

Holness enrolled in California State University, in Los Angeles, where he majored in electrical engineering. At the same time, he began performing stand-up at local comedy clubs. Four years later Ned won an open mike competition at the Laugh

Factory. Certain he could earn a living making people laugh, he left school in 1989, just a few credits short of graduating.

GOODBYE NED HOLNESS

Success in the local comedy clubs brought Ned to the attention of Mitzi Shore, owner of a world famous club called the Comedy Store. She believed he could make it as a Latino comic, but that he needed to change his name. He decided to adopt the name Carlos Mencia for his stage character, in honor of his mother. And he began to appear regularly at the Comedy Store.

Mencia developed a distinctive, no-holds-barred, confrontational style of humor that led to an appearance on *Buscando Estrellas*, a Latino version of the amateur talent show competition *Star Search*. There, he earned the title of International Comedy Grand Champion.

Subsequent appearances on television soon followed. Mencia appeared on *The Arsenio Hall Show, In Living Color, Moesha*, and *An Evening at the Improv*. He also hosted the HBO comedy series *Loco Slam,* in 1994, and the Galavision show *Funny Is Funny!* in 1998.

Mencia performs at the historic Orpheum Theater in Los Angeles.

FINDING SUCCESS

Mencia released his first comedy album—*Take a Joke, America*—in 2000. The following year, he toured with Freddy Soto and Pablo Francisco as a member of the frequently sold-out Three Amigos comedy tour. Highlights from the tour were later included in a best-selling DVD.

Carlos Mencia: Comedian

In September 2007 Carlos Mencia and his wife, Amy, arrive at the premiere of The Heartbreak Kid *at Mann's Village Theater, in Los Angeles.*

Carlos made several cable television appearances. He performed on *HBO Comedy Half-Hour*, for which he later received a Cable-ACE (Award for Cable Excellence) nomination for Best Stand-Up Comedy Special. He followed up with a performance on the popular series *Comedy Central Presents*. It wasn't long after that Comedy Central offered him his own show.

Mind of Mencia premiered in July 2005. The show, which features a combination of stand-up comedy, skits, and man-in-the-street interviews, quickly proved to be a hit. In 2006 it was Comedy Central's second-highest rated program, eclipsed only by the animated series *South Park*.

The year 2006 was also exciting in Mencia's private life. His son, Lucas Pablo, was born that December. It was the first child for Carlos and his wife, Amy, who were married in 2003.

In announcing plans to renew *Mind of Mencia* for a third season, Lauren Corrao, executive vice president of original programming and development, said, "Mencia has proven to be a true break-out star who's incredibly popular with our viewers and a huge asset to our network. Renewing this series was a very easy decision for us and we are excited to be a part of the rapid growth of the Carlos Mencia brand." The network later renewed the show for a fourth season, which began in May 2008.

ACCUSATIONS

Carlos's success brought him more and more fans, but also critics as well. Several comedians accused him of stealing material from other comics. The accusations against Mencia came to a head in February 2007 when he and comic Joe Rogan argued onstage at the Comedy Store.

Carlos has denied the charges that he has plagiarized the work of other comedians and refuses to let the comments affect his act. He says,

> When you become popular, there's always going to be varying opinions about it. Honestly, once you start thinking about stuff like that and editing yourself and questioning your thoughts and ideas—it would be like [the impressionist artist] Monet had said, 'You know, somebody already did a painting with flowers. I'm not going to do any more of that.' It's my art and I do what I think is funny. I write what I think is funny.

Despite the controversy Carlos's career continued on an upward path. He starred opposite Ben Stiller and Michelle Monaghan in the feature film *The Heartbreak Kid*, which was released in October 2007. The movie was a hit at the box office on its opening weekend, earning an estimated $14 million. However critics gave the film mixed reviews.

That same year, from September to December, Mencia appeared in sold-out comedy tours in cities across the country. Afterward he entertained the troops in the Persian Gulf while on a USO tour.

◄ **CROSS-CURRENTS** ►

Immigration is a common topic in Carlos Mencia's comedy routines. To read what he has to say on the subject, turn to page 52.

As of late 2008 Mencia's calendar has remained full as his faithful fans in cities across the country flock to see the no-holds-barred comedian in his second comedy tour. The Carlos Mencia phenomenon shows no signs of letting up any time soon.

Carlos Mencia: Comedian

CHAPTER FIVE

Christy Turlington: Supermodel and Entrepreneur

Christy Turlington first came into the public eye during the 1980s as a teenage model. Of Salvadoran descent, she was one of the first models to gain international acclaim as a celebrity. In the years that followed she served as a spokeswoman and fashion icon. But she also parlayed her fame into a career on the business side of the fashion industry, as a founder of companies selling skin care products and clothing.

FAME AT AN EARLY AGE

Christy Nicole Turlington was the second of three daughters born to Dwain Turlington and María Elizabeth Parker. Her father was an American who worked as an airline pilot and her mother, who was from El Salvador, was a flight attendant. The Turlingtons lived in the San Francisco suburb of Walnut Creek, California, where Christy was born on January 2, 1969. She spent most of her childhood in Danville, California, where she and her younger sister, Erin, and older sister, Kelly, were raised.

In the 1980s the family moved temporarily to Miami, Florida. In 1982 14-year-old Christy was horseback riding at a stable in Florida with her sister Kelly when fashion photographer Dennie Cody asked them both to pose for a

Christy Turlington models a gown during a 1998 charity auction. A savvy businesswoman today, the supermodel is widely respected in the fashion industry.

photo shoot. Christy was later asked to sign on with an agency as a model.

At age 15 Christy was modeling part-time. She appeared in a series of successful ads for a store called Emporium Capwell. Christy's elegant beauty quickly made her a photographer favorite. Because her parents insisted that she finish school before modeling full-time, she was limited to working after school and during the summers. Christy recalled in an interview, "I never thought modeling was cool. But it gave me freedom. I got to travel and I earned money. I don't know that I ever felt comfortable with it, though. It's a derailing thing to be 15 years old, given lots of money and flown around the world."

After graduating from Monte Vista High School, in Danville, California, Christy moved to New York City to model full-time. Her career took off after famous modeling scout Eileen Ford got her a 1987 cover shoot for *Vogue Italy*. Turlington also appeared in 1987 on the covers of *Cosmopolitan* and *Esquire* and signed a cosmetic contract with Revlon.

The 1990s were the decade of the supermodels— celebrity fashion icons who represented top fashion designers and labels. This 1995 photo shows four elite models of the time: from left to right, Naomi Campbell, Claudia Schiffer, Christy Turlington, and Elle Macpherson.

SUPERMODEL

In 1989 Christy signed a contract with fashion designer Calvin Klein to promote his company's Eternity fragrance. Klein explained her appeal: "I chose [Christy] early on when she was very young because I thought she represented quality and intelligence. She has all of the qualities that she ended up representing in our Eternity [perfume] campaign—about family and children. That's what she's really all about."

Christy followed up her deal with Calvin Klein by signing with Maybelline to become the cosmetic giant's spokesperson. By that time, she was known as one of the five original supermodels. The other four were Naomi Campbell, Cindy Crawford, Linda Evangelista, and Claudia Schiffer.

During the late 1980s and the 1990s Christy was on hundreds of covers and featured in the print ads of numerous fashion and style magazines, including *Vogue* and *Elle*. She also appeared in music videos for pop musician George Michael and the rock band Duran Duran. And she played herself in several television films about the fashion industry.

THE SPIRITUAL SIDE OF LIFE

In 1994, at age 25, Turlington retired from modeling after a decade in the business. The next year, she joined forces with Naomi Campbell, Claudia Schiffer, and Elle MacPherson in opening the Fashion Café restaurant in New York City. Two other outlets were later opened in London, England, and Barcelona, Spain.

After retiring from modeling, Turlington enrolled in the Gallatin School of Individualized Study at New York University, in New York City, where she combined an interest in religion and longtime practice of yoga in her studies. In 1999 she obtained a bachelor of arts degree in comparative religion and Eastern philosophy. Three years later she wrote *Living Yoga: Creating a Life Practice.*

Turlington has said that her interest in spiritual matters has helped her find peace of mind in a hectic world. She has followed her interests in founding three companies: The first—a skincare line called Sundari—was started in 1999. The following year, she joined with the sportswear firm Puma to start two clothing lines: Nuala and Mahanuala, the latter of which features yogawear. Although she and her partners sold Sundari in 2003, she continues to look for ways to help the two clothing lines expand their business.

During the 1990s Christy was romantically linked with different men, including screenwriter Roger Wilson and actors Christian Slater and Jason Patric. In June 2003 she married writer, director, and actor Ed Burns. Their daughter, Grace, was born in October 2003 and their son, Finn, was born in February 2006.

Christy appears with sister Kelly at the 2003 Sundance Film Festival. The three Turlington sisters— Christy, Kelly, and Erin—have had a close relationship since childhood.

ADVOCACY EFFORTS

In addition to working as a businesswoman, Christy has also taken on various causes, including serving as an antismoking activist. She smoked on and off from age 13 to 28. But in 1997, after her father died at age 63 from lung cancer, she was determined to quit. After she succeeded, she began working with the Centers for Disease Control, making public service announcements and print ads about smoking cessation and lung cancer awareness. She also created a Web site called SmokingIsUgly.com. It serves as an online resource for anyone interested in quitting smoking or learning about lung cancer. In an interview with *Psychology Today* Christy explained:

> I have learned that I can be most effective through my anti-tobacco work. It has been great because it has turned so many personal negatives into positives for me. I was addicted to tobacco for many years and then lost my father to lung cancer due to his addiction to the substance. Now I can share my experience and struggle and encourage others to take better care of themselves.

◄ CROSS-CURRENTS ►

Studies have shown that government bans on smoking in public places have helped inspire people to try to stop smoking. For more information on such bans, turn to page 53.

Turlington is also involved with several other charities and volunteer organizations. She says she holds a special spot in her heart for organizations that focus on the needs of women and children. "Anything to do with children being hungry or not getting the medication they need," she said. "The idea of a mother not being able to keep herself alive to give her kids medicine. Those are the things I'm most passionate about."

Some of her volunteer efforts have taken Christy to places outside the United States. She has traveled to her mother's birthplace, El Salvador, as an advocate for maternal health for the international relief organization CARE. And she has traveled to Swaziland as part of the (RED) Campaign, the effort to eliminate AIDS in Africa.

Christy has published a calendar of her photos and donates the proceeds from sales to the American Foundation for El Salvador, an organization that aids the poor. Christy also gives her support to Fashion Targets Breast Cancer and People for the Ethical Treatment of Animals (PETA).

CHAPTER SIX

Mariano Rivera: Pro Baseball Player

I n the history of Major League Baseball only five players who made their reputations as relief pitchers have been elected to the Baseball Hall of Fame, in Cooperstown, New York. One of these is Dennis Eckersley, who says there is no question about who is the best relief pitcher to ever take

the mound: It's Mariano Rivera. "The best ever, no doubt about it," says Eckersley. Rivera, the slender righthander from Panama, has been a dominant figure for the New York Yankees, not only during the regular season, but also in postseason play.

PLAYING BASEBALL

Mariano "Mo" Rivera was born on November 29, 1969, in Panama City, Panama. Rivera's father was a fisherman

New York Yankees pitcher Mariano Rivera tips his hat to the fans at the last game of the 2008 regular season at Yankee Stadium. Since 1997 the relief pitcher has been the Yankees closer—the pitcher responsible for getting the final outs of the game.

who spent long hours at sea working to support his children—Mariano also had two brothers, Alvaro and Giraldo, and a sister, Delia. Mariano credits his father with making him the person he is today. "If it wasn't for him," says Rivera, "I don't think I would have this character. His character is strong, and he taught me that way."

Mariano learned the game of baseball as a child in Panama. However, he had to provide his own equipment: He cut up cardboard to make gloves and used tree branches and broomsticks for bats.

The young boy lived in the small village of Puerto Caimito, where he sometimes helped his father work as a fisherman. One day when Mariano was 18, he was on a boat that capsized. He saved himself by jumping into another boat. The incident convinced him that he was not cut out to follow in his father's footsteps.

In 1989 Rivera was playing shortstop for Panama Oeste (West Panama). The team's pitcher had given a disappointing performance in a previous game, so Mariano volunteered to pitch. His teammates were so impressed with his pitching that they recommended him to a Yankees scout named Chico Heron. Heron came to see Mariano play, and recommended to

The modern skyscrapers of Panama City, where Rivera was born. He grew up about 20 miles to the west, in a small commercial fishing village on the Pacific Coast called Puerto Caimito.

◀ **CROSS-CURRENTS** ▶

Another baseball player born in Panama who went on to great success in the major leagues was infielder Rod Carew. To read his story, turn to page 54.

In 2008 Mariano Rivera held the Major League Baseball record for most postseason saves (34) and most World Series saves (9).

Yankees executive Herb Raybourn that the team sign the 20 year old. The $3,000 deal was completed on February 17, 1990.

THE ROAD TO NEW YORK

Mariano began his professional career in 1991 at the lowest level of the minors (Class A) with the Greensboro Hornets of the Class A South Atlantic League. He had two successful seasons in the low minors before suffering an arm injury that required surgery. In 1993 he returned to action and continued to make a push towards the majors. In 1994 he played for each minor league team of the Yankees: single A in Tampa, Florida; AA at Albany, New York; and AAA at Columbus, Ohio.

Following an impressive season in 1994, Rivera was called up to the majors in 1995. But he had an inconsistent debut as a starting pitcher, and was sent back to the minors. The Yankees were so unhappy with his performance that they almost traded him to the Detroit Tigers. However, in one minor league start Rivera demonstrated his potential when the velocity of his fastball reached 95 and 96 miles per hour on the radar gun. Yankees' management reconsidered, and decided against the deal. It proved to be one of the best trades the team never made.

After being brought back up to the majors Rivera enjoyed significant success over the second half of the 1995 season and in the 1995 American League championship series. By the end of the postseason the team had decided his future was in the bullpen as a relief pitcher.

A STAR IS BORN

In 1996 Mariano proved to be a reliable relief pitcher, usually coming in the inning before closer John Wetteland. In the postseason that fall, he went 1–0 with a 0.63 earned run average in 14⅓ innings pitched. Rivera earned his first World Series ring when he helped New York defeat the Atlanta Braves in the 1996 World Series. His performance impressed the team so much that the Yankees let Wetteland leave as a free agent after the season, making Rivera the new closer.

From 1997 through 2008 Mariano put together one magnificent season after another. In his first full year as closer, he was named to the All-Star Game and saved the midsummer classic for the American League. The 1997 postseason, however, included a moment that was arguably a low point of Rivera's career. With the Yankees only four outs away from advancing to the American League championship series, Mariano blew a save against the Cleveland Indians. Cleveland bounced back to defeat New York and send the Yankees home for the winter.

Mariano rebounded the next year, saving 36 games in the regular season. In the postseason he had three saves as the Yankees posted a four-game sweep of the San Diego Padres and collected their second World Series championship in three years.

THE CUT FASTBALL

In 1999 Mariano developed a new pitch: a cut fastball, or cutter. The pitch comes in straight until the last second, when it breaks down and away from a righthanded batter. It became a devastating weapon in Rivera's arsenal of pitches. Even when hitters knew it was coming, they couldn't do anything with it. Whether the pitch is a two-seam fastball, changeup, or a cutter, Chicago White Sox slugger Jim Thome says, "Mariano's pitch is the best ever in the history of the game."

Rivera saved 45 games during the 1999 season and then followed up with a superb postseason. He was named Most

Valuable Player as the Yankees won the 1999 World Series by sweeping the Braves in four straight games.

Rivera continued to dominate hitters year after year. He allowed just 2 earned runs in over 51 innings played in the American League Division Series from 1995 through the 2001. In 2001 and 2004 Mariano saved more than 50 games in each season, a remarkable achievement for a relief pitcher. As of 2008 in postseason play (76 games), he had saved a record 34 games with an earned run average of 0.77, both major league records. At the time he was ranked second, behind Trevor Hoffman, on the all-time saves list.

Mariano and his wife, Clara, have three sons. Eleven-year-old Mariano (left) and eight-year-old Jafet appear with their parents in this July 2005 photograph. Two-year-old Jaziel was born in November 2002.

AWARDS AND HONORS

In 14 major league seasons, Mariano has been selected for nine All-Star Games. In addition to his MVP award in the 1999 World Series, he was also named Most Valuable Player of the 2003 American League Championship Series. In addition, he has won four Rolaids Relief awards as the league's top relief pitcher.

In November 2007 the Yankees signed Rivera to a three-year, $45 million contract that makes him the highest-paid closer in big league history. His value to the team cannot be measured by just wins and saves, however. He has been praised not only for his athletic abilities, but also for serving as a role model and mentor for others, including younger pitchers trying to make it to the majors. When Mariano decides to hang up his glove, he will undoubtedly join baseball's greats in the sport's Hall of Fame in Cooperstown, New York.

CHAPTER SEVEN

Christianne Meneses Jacobs: Magazine Founder

Christianne Meneses Jacobs is the founder and editor of a Spanish-language magazine for children. A native of Managua, Nicaragua, who is married to a U.S. citizen, she decided that the way to educate her American-born children about their mother's heritage was to create *Iguana*, an educational magazine for children living in the United States. It was first published in 2005.

FLIGHT FROM NICARAGUA

Christianne Meneses was born into a prosperous family in Managua, Nicaragua, on March 28, 1971. In July 1979, when she was eight years old, the Sandinistas seized power in the country. Although the socialist group had promised democracy, it established a

Magazine founder Christianne Meneses Jacobs is honored at the Anna Maria Arias Memorial Business Fund 2007 Gala Awards. Named in honor of the late founder of Latina Style *magazine, the awards recognize the accomplishments of Hispanic women.*

military junta to rule the country. Christianne's father, Enrique, who was an internationally known lawyer, was very involved in the fight for democracy in the Sandinista-controlled country. He was jailed several times for his work.

In 1988, after Enrique had defended an American against spy charges, the Meneses family no longer felt safe living in Nicaragua. At age 17 Christianne fled with her father, mother, and brother to Los Angeles, California. They were forced to leave all their possessions behind, and entered the United States with just $500. In an interview Christianne talked about the sudden change in the family's lives: "One day you are rich and you are affluent . . . and you have maids, cooks, a driver and nannies. And the next day, you come to this country and you are poor and you have nothing."

A view of the city of Los Angeles. Christianne was 17 years old when she and her family moved from Nicaragua to California.

MAKING A NEW LIFE

In order to make money, the lawyer and his wife took jobs as luggage checkers at Los Angeles International Airport. The jobs did not pay well. Christianne would later comment on how hard it was for them to support her and her brother on less than $20,000 a year.

Christianne had studied English since she was nine years old, but at Los Angeles High School she had the opportunity to improve her language skills. She excelled in school and became interested in journalism. She eventually became editor-in-chief of the school's Spanish and English newspapers.

After graduating from high school with honors, Christianne received a

NICARAGUA

Located between Honduras and Costa Rica, and bordering both the Caribbean Sea and the North Pacific Ocean, Nicaragua is the largest nation in Central America. Around 5.8 million live in the country, which is slightly smaller than the state of New York. The capital city of Nicaragua is Managua.

four-year scholarship at Wesleyan University, in Middletown, Connecticut. There, she majored in government, with a concentration on international relations. Afterward she took a job as a bilingual second grade teacher at Union Avenue Elementary School, in Los Angeles.

Meneses continued taking college classes while teaching, and received her master of arts in education in 2001. Four years later, she received her certification as a reading specialist. Meanwhile, she met and married graphics artist Marc Jacobs. The couple had a daughter they named Isabelle Celene. In 2002 they moved to Phoenix, Arizona, where Christianne Jacobs continues to teach elementary school.

FILLING A NEED

Christianne wanted her daughter grow up speaking both English and Spanish, and to develop an appreciation for her Nicaraguan heritage. In order to encourage this, she spoke only Spanish to the child at home, while Marc spoke only English.

When Isabelle was around two years old, Christianne realized that there were very few original Spanish books that she could use to teach her daughter to read—and learn about the Latin American culture. Most Spanish-language books that were available were translations of kids' books written originally in English. Christianne and Marc were inspired to do something to fill this need by publishing a magazine. She explained:

> My husband and I realized that a magazine could deliver a variety of original Spanish-language materials for parents. We researched the idea for over a year. Many librarians and teachers told us that they had never seen a Spanish-language children's magazine and enthusiastically embraced our idea.

Christianne poses with several of her magazine's namesakes. The name Iguana was chosen for her magazine because the word is the same in English and Spanish.

IGUANA

The Jacobs settled on the name Iguana for their new publication. Christianne explained the rationale for the name:

> We thought it was a good idea to use a word that can be spelled the same way both in English and Spanish. Besides, I grew up in a tropical country, Nicaragua, where every day at noon all the iguanas living in our backyard would come out to take sun baths.

With Marc as art director and Christianne as editor, *Iguana* debuted with a 10-page sample issue in 2004. The premiere issue was published in May 2005.

The magazine is aimed at kids ages 7 through 12. It features a variety of content: pieces of fiction, poetry, biographies, craft projects, puzzles, contests, and more. In addition, Jacobs has said, the magazine is intended to introduce kids to topics that schools do not typically cover in much detail. She explains:

> Our students are only taught the basics in schools while general culture is neglected. . . . *Iguana* contains various sections such as Inventions that Changed the World, Mythology, Children Around the World (with history and geography) and a feature on exotic animals, recipes, arts and crafts and comic strips. One of my favorite features is the interview section in which I select a successful Latino/a who can be a role model for Latino children.

Reaction to *Iguana* has been favorable. For her efforts in starting up the magazine, Christianne was honored in 2007 with an award of $5,000 from the Anna Maria Arias Memorial Business Fund. Presented by *Latina Style* magazine, the award recognizes Latinas for their innovation, achievement and community service.

In addition to serving as president of her company, NicaGal, and publisher of two magazines, Jacobs also works as a first grade teacher.

Iguana magazine is published by a company that Jacobs founded called NicaGal. It is based in Scottsdale, Arizona. In August 2007 NicaGal announced it would be producing a new free monthly magazine called *Yo Sé!*—(Spanish for "I know"). The new magazine, which debuted in early 2008, is aimed at older kids and teens. It features Spanish-language articles on popular culture including stories on movies and television shows and interviews with Latino personalities, especially those who are making an impact in U.S. society. The publication is distributed for free in Spanish-language newspapers based in Los Angeles, Chicago, and other cities.

◀ CROSS-CURRENTS ▶

The Jacobs cofounded *Iguana* to help their child be bilingual—fluent in English and Spanish. Bilingual programs are sometimes used to help non-English speaking school students. To learn more, turn to page 54.

America Ferrera: Actress

America Ferrera has become famous as the braces-wearing star of the hit television sitcom *Ugly Betty*. Born of Honduran parents, the California native has also starred in several feature films. Her success inspired *Time* magazine to name her as one of the Most Influential People in the World for 2007.

CALIFORNIA GIRL

America Georgine Ferrera was born on April 18, 1984, in Los Angeles, California. Her parents, who were born in Honduras, immigrated to the United States in the mid-1970s. America was given the same name as her mother (a name that she has told interviewers is not at all uncommon in Latin America).

America is the youngest in a family of six children—five girls and one

Actress America Ferrera was one of many celebrities attending the Glamour *magazine Women of the Year Awards held in November 2008, in New York City.*

boy. When she was seven years old her parents divorced, and her father returned to Honduras. She has not seen him since he left. Her mother became the family's sole support. She raised the children in Woodland Hills, a district of the city of Los Angeles, while working as the manager of a hotel cleaning staff.

From an early age Ferrera knew that she wanted to act. She told one interviewer that she got her first chance while still a little girl:

> My very first encounter with acting happened when I was seven: My sisters were auditioning for the junior high school play and I begged them to take me with them; they were like, 'You're too young, you can't be in the play.' But the director thought I was cute and cast me.

America's mother was not convinced that the acting profession was a good career choice for her daughter. She had always stressed the importance of an education to her children, all of whom would eventually graduate from college.

America pursued roles in school plays and joined the California Youth Theatre in Hollywood when she was 11. Her mother did not support the budding actress so she was forced to take public transportation to get to the auditions. Eventually America's mother became convinced of her daughter's dedication and would drive her to West Hollywood for the auditions.

A BIG BREAK

America signed with a talent agency when she was 16 years old. The next year, she got the break for which every aspiring actor and actress hopes. While still a student at El Camino Real High School in Woodland Hills, she won a role in the 2002 Disney Channel movie of the week *Gotta Kick It Up*.

In the film America played a Latina youngster who becomes part of a championship dance troupe. "I love to dance," relates America," so I couldn't believe I was getting paid to just dance all day. And there were four other girls in the cast, so that was fun. And you know the way you think when you're a teenager: Disney Channel today, Oscars tomorrow!"

Ferrera's performance in the movie impressed the right people. She won the lead role in the HBO production *Real Women Have Curves*. She portrayed a young girl who pursues her dream of a writing career, despite opposition from the character's mother. America's performance earned her a Sundance award—the Special Jury Prize for Acting. She was also nominated for a Young Artist Award for best performance in a feature film and for an Independent Spirit Award for best debut performance.

In order to pursue her acting career America had delayed going to college. But she remembered her mother's words about the importance of education. She enrolled at the University of Southern California, where she studied for a double major in theater and international relations. While there, fellow student Ryan Piers Williams cast her in a film. The two began dating during production of the movie and have remained a couple ever since.

With these credits on her résumé, America landed an appearance on the popular CBS television show *Touched by an Angel*. After that, she earned parts in the Hallmark Hall of Fame production *Plainsong* (2004) and on an episode of *CSI: Crime Scene Investigation*. America also costarred in the 2005 drama *The Sisterhood of the Traveling Pants*, which is based on a popular book series written by Ann Brashares.

A scene from Real Women Have Curves. *In the 2002 film America played a Mexican-American teenager in conflict with her traditional parents. They want her to stay home to help support the family—and not go off to college.*

America Ferrera: Actress

Actresses from The Sisterhood of the Traveling Pants *pose at the June 2005 Los Angeles premiere. From left to right are Alexis Bledel, Blake Lively, America Ferrera, and Amber Tamblyn.*

UGLY BETTY

While attending a film festival, America met actress Salma Hayek. Soon after, Hayek contacted her to discuss a new project she was involved in. It was a remake of a popular Colombian television series called *Yo Soy Betty, la Fea.*

America auditioned for—and won—the role of the lead character Betty Suarez. Betty is an assistant at a fashion magazine. She is unattractive, especially in the eyes of her fashion-conscious peers at the magazine. But she has a heart of gold. Ferrera explained to *Latina Magazine* why she was attracted to the role of Betty:

> You just loved her because of her eternal optimism. She did not want to be pitied; she did not pity herself.

Ferrera's performance as the hardworking fashion assistant in Ugly Betty *has made her a household name.*

Everything she took with a little sense of humor. She had dignity. She was like, 'I know what people think I am, but I'm not going to let that stop me from being a happy person and having a happy life.' That's fun to watch. You want to root for somebody that does that for themselves.

Ugly Betty debuted in 2006 and was an immediate hit. America became a celebrity. For her role as Betty she won the 2007 Golden Globe Award for Best Actress in a Comedy Series. She also received the 2007 Screen Actors Guild award for Outstanding Performance by a Female Actor in a Comedy Series and an Emmy for Best Actress in a Comedy Series.

America's honors were not limited to the field of entertainment. A California member of the House of Representatives congratulated Ferrera during a legislative session for serving as a role model for young Latinas. She was also named to *People* magazine's 100 Most Beautiful list.

In 2007 Lloyd's of London insured America's vibrant smile for $10 million. With her new film, *The Sisterhood of the Traveling Pants 2*, released in the summer of 2008, and the continued success of *Ugly Betty*, she has a lot to smile about.

◀ **CROSS-CURRENTS** ▶

Ugly Betty is broadcast during television's primetime viewing hours. For additional information on how the viewing habits of people watching primetime television have changed over the years, turn to page 55.

ATTITUDES TOWARD IMMIGRATION

The Gallup Organization surveys people around the world to determine public opinion regarding various political, social, and economic issues. One issue that Gallup has researched over the years is immigration to the United States. In general, Americans have a positive view of immigration, reports the Gallup Web site:

> Three in four [Americans] have consistently said it has been good for the United States in the past, and a majority says it is good for the nation today. However, Americans still seem interested in limiting the amount of immigration.

When asked in a July 2008 Gallup survey about the level of immigration into the United States, 39 percent of Americans favored decreasing the number of immigrants allowed into the country, a decrease from 45 percent a year earlier. However, only 18 percent believe it should be increased.

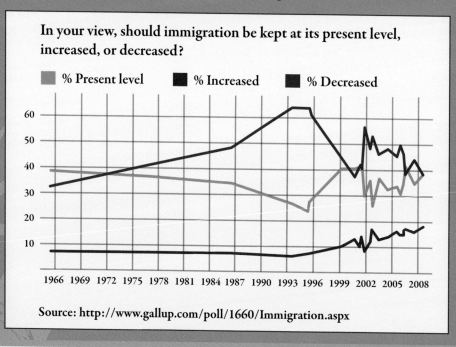

In your view, should immigration be kept at its present level, increased, or decreased?

■ % Present level   ■ % Increased   ■ % Decreased

Source: http://www.gallup.com/poll/1660/Immigration.aspx

SUPPORTING THE SPACE PROGRAM

Since the mid-1970s, when the first space shuttle was being built, the National Aeronautics and Space Administration budget has ranged from $3 to $17 billion per year. NASA is federally funded, which means its budget comes from tax dollars paid by U.S. citizens. Despite the expense, most Americans have favorable opinions about the space agency.

When a September 14–16, 2007, Gallup poll asked Americans to rate NASA, 56 percent rated the organization positively: 16 percent said it was doing an "excellent" job and 40 percent said "good." Only 8 percent said "poor," while the rest reported "only fair." According to Gallup, these opinions are similar to numbers reported in previous years: In 2006, 57 percent of respondents reported positive ratings for NASA. The previous year 53 percent and 60 percent gave positive ratings in two separate polls.

For the most part the public has given the agency positive evaluations since 1990, when the question was first asked by Gallup. More negative marks came in July 1990, after scientists discovered a flaw in the Hubble telescope (when only 46 percent gave NASA an excellent or good rating). Only 43 percent gave positive feedback in September 1993, when a poll was taken soon after NASA lost contact with a Mars orbiter and after several space shuttle missions were cancelled.

NASA's John F. Kennedy Space Center, located in Brevard County, Florida, is the launch site for the space shuttle and the landing site for the orbiter.

THE *SPORTS ILLUSTRATED* COVER JINX

Over the years the idea that an athlete's appearance on the cover of *Sports Illustrated* magazine can cause bad luck has gained in popularity. In the game following his appearance on the cover Rolando Blackman recorded 21 points and 10 rebounds in Kansas State's loss to North Carolina in the West Regional Final of the NCAA Tournament. Since North Carolina was favored in the game and Blackman played well, it did not appear that he had been jinxed in any way.

In 2002, the magazine editors conducted a search to determine if a jinx really existed. They researched what happened to every athlete who had been featured on the cover since the magazine's inception in 1954. In investigating almost all of the 2,456 covers up to that time, they found 913 cases of what they termed jinxes—"a demonstrable misfortune or decline in performance following a cover appearance." That works out to a so-called jinx occurring approximately 37 percent of the time.

The theory about the magazine cover jinx dates back to the magazine's very first cover subject, slugger Eddie Mathews of the Milwaukee Braves. Exactly one week after appearing on the magazine cover Mathews suffered a hand injury that caused him to miss several games. Many other players and teams have suffered injuries or losses in the 54 years since then, some more serious than others.

CARLOS MENCIA AND THE IMMIGRATION DEBATE

Carlos Mencia is well known for making comments in his standup comedy about many aspects of immigration, including Latino assimilation in American society, language barriers (Spanish versus English), and illegal immigration. His comedy includes racially charged jokes and insults as well as statements on the Hispanic culture and its place in American society.

In his remarks, Mencia often pokes fun of both sides of the immigration debate. In a 2003 interview with CNN, for example, he commented on why he is able to have this perspective:

I see the world from a prism that is unique in the sense that, you know, I was born in Honduras, but my mom's Mexican. I grew up in east L.A. where everybody's Mexican. But I kind of got treated like an insider and outsider at the same time. I'm an American, but I don't always get treated like one. And so I'm kind of able to see things from two angles, you know what I mean?

Mencia has said that he appreciates living in a country where he can be a controversial comedian. In a 2007 interview he explained: "I grew up being very patriotic. My parents really love this country. A big part of what they love is freedom of speech. . . . I'm fearless because aren't we supposed to be able to speak our mind?"

Research has shown that tobacco use can cause deaths and diseases such as lung cancer, emphysema, heart disease, and various chronic conditions. Smoking is responsible for almost one out of three cancer deaths. It is estimated that heavy smokers have reduced their life expectancy by as much as seven or eight years. In addition, secondhand smoke has been proven to cause health problems in nonsmokers who live with smokers.

A July 2008 Gallup poll reported that most people agree with the scientific evidence. Almost 82 percent said they believe that smoking is very harmful, while almost 14 percent said that it is somewhat harmful. Only about 1.5 percent of respondents said that smoking is not at all harmful.

The antismoking movement got its start in the 1970s, when the city of Berkeley, California, banned smoking from restaurants, bars, and other public places. As of 2007, 22 states had enacted tough antismoking laws. At the same time Gallup polls reported that increasing numbers of people believed that smoking in public places should be made illegal: 31 percent in 2003, 39 percent in 2005, and almost 40 percent in 2007. The percentage of those who thought smoking should be outlawed completely dropped from about 15.5 percent in 2003 and 2005 to just under 12 percent in 2007.

Christy Turlington has served as a spokesperson for the American Cancer Society's Great American Smokeout. The annual smoking cessation event, held the third Thursday in November, calls for smokers to give up the habit for at least 24 hours.

ROD CAREW

Rodney Cline "Rod" Carew was born to a Panamanian mother in the town of Gatún, Panama. At age 14, he came to the United States and his family settled in Manhattan, in New York City. After graduating from George Washington High School, Carew signed with the Minnesota Twins.

Carew proved his value to the Twins right from the start. In 1967 he was named the American League's Rookie of the Year and an All-Star. In the years that followed he would be selected as an All-Star 17 more times.

The MLB player remained with the Twins for 12 seasons before moving on to seven more years with the California Angels. He had a lifetime batting average of .328 and he averaged better than .300 for 15 consecutive seasons. In 1985 he reached the 3,000-hit mark.

During his career Rod Carew won many awards, including the Roberto Clemente Award, given to the player who best exemplifies the games of baseball, sportsmanship, and community involvement. Upon his retirement, both teams retired his uniform number (number 29). In 1991 he was voted into Baseball's Hall of Fame on the first ballot.

Carew remained active in baseball after retiring. He founded the Rod Carew Baseball School, which provides instruction to major league teams and players. He also worked for the Angels and Milwaukee Brewers as a hitting instructor before taking a job working on the executive staff of the Minnesota Twins.

LEARNING ENGLISH

Iguana publishers Christianne Meneses Jacobs and her husband, Marc, are raising their children to be fluent in two languages, or bilingual. Toward that end, Christianne speaks to them only in Spanish at home, while her husband speaks to them only in English. Many immigrant children who come to the United States are not bilingual—and they can have a difficult time learning English.

In education, there are two thoughts on how to educate non-English speaking students: immersion or bilingual programs. Immersion refers to quickly immersing students in English-only classes so they can join regular classes within a year. A bilingual program provides instruction in the person's native language as well as in English. Bilingual programs can be expensive and it can be difficult for public school systems to fund and provide teachers fluent in many different languages. Some states, like California, Arizona, and Massachusetts, have eliminated bilingual programs.

Supporters of bilingual education point out that fluency in more than one language is a great asset. Pedro Ruíz, president of the National Association for Bilingual Education in Washington, told the *Christian Science Monitor*: "We want to compete in the global market right now, and the only way to do that is with kids who have embraced another language early on."

PRIMETIME TELEVISION

The term *primetime* refers to the hours in the evening when television viewing is at its peak. In the Eastern and Pacific time zones, primetime is from 7:00 P.M to 11:00 P.M.; in the Central and Mountain time zones, it is from 6:00 P.M to 10:00 P.M. Research has shown that over the past 50 years primetime viewing habits have changed drastically.

From television's early days through the 1960s, there were three major networks (CBS, NBC, and ABC). Together, they attracted 80 percent to 90 percent of the primetime viewing audience. However, the emergence of videocassette recorders and the growth of cable television gave viewers a wider range of viewing options. Because viewers were no longer limited in what they could watch during primetime, their viewing habits changed. By the 1990s the three networks' share of the viewing audience had dropped to around 60 percent to 65 percent.

New technologies have continued to expand the number of viewing options even further. In a 2008 Integrated Media Measurement study of teens and adults, 20 percent of those responding said they use their computer to watch some primetime programs online. According to the study about half of those were using the computer as a substitute for the television set. The survey reported that 13- to -24-year-olds accounted for only 19.1 percent of the online viewers, while 25- to 44-year-olds made up 58.4 percent of the online audience.

NOTES

CHAPTER 1

p. 10: "require immigrants who . . ." Joseph Carroll, "Hispanics Support Requiring English Proficiency for Immigrants," Gallup, July 5, 2007. http://www.gallup.com/poll/28048/Hispanics-Support-Requiring-English-Proficiency-Immigrants.aspx

CHAPTER 2

p. 14: "What I really wanted to . . ." Quoted in Jim H. Smith, "Reaching for Distant Moons . . . and Beyond," *UConn Traditions*, Fall/Winter 2002. http://uconnmagazine.uconn.edu/fwin2002/fwin02f1.html

p. 15: "I had lots of powerful . . ." Quoted in Joseph D'Agnese, "The Boy NASA Couldn't Keep on Earth," *Discover*, November 8, 2003. http://discovermagazine.com/2003/nov/space-explorer

p. 16: "The objective is to travel . . ." Quoted in Smith, "Reaching for Distant Moons . . . and Beyond."

CHAPTER 3

p. 18: "because it was quiet and . . ." Quoted in Vic Ziegel, "Someday, Blackman Will Have a Team of His Own," *Daily News*, February 7, 2001.

p. 22: "I knew I was intelligent . . ." Quoted in Talia Bargil, "Where Are They Now? Rolando Blackman," Legends of Basketball: National Basketball Retired Players Association, January 31,

2006. https://www.nbrpa.com/news/wherenow/rolando_blackman.aspx

CHAPTER 4

p. 24: "My birth father had built . . ." Quoted in Carl Kozlowski, "Carlos Mencia Just Said That," *LA City Beat*, March 29, 2007. http://www.lacitybeat.com/cms/story/detail/carlos_mencia_just_said_that/5264/

p. 26: "Mencia has proven to be . . ." Quoted in "Comedy Central Delves Deeper into the 'Mind of Mencia' and Orders Third Season," *Comedy Central* news release, July 12, 2006. http://www.futoncritic.com/news.aspx?id=20060712comedycentral01

p. 27: "When you become popular, there's . . ." Quoted in John Wenzel, "Comedy Q&A: Carlos Mencia," *Get Real Denver*, July 25, 2008. http://www.getrealdenver.com/2008/07/25/comedy-qa-carlos-mencia/

CHAPTER 5

p. 29: "I never thought modeling was . . ." Quoted in "Christy Turlington: The Outsider," *Telegraph*, September 23, 2007. http://www.telegraph.co.uk/fashion/main.jhtml?xml=/fashion/2007/09/23/st_christyturlington.xml&page=1

p. 29: "I chose her early on . . ." Quoted in "Christy Turlington: The Outsider."

p. 32: "I have learned that I . . ." Quoted in Michael Seeber, "Christy Turlington: Beauty and Balance,"

Psychology Today, July/August 2001. http://psychologytoday.com/articles/index.php?term=pto-20010701-000022&print=1

p. 32: "Anything to do with children . . ." Quoted in Jenny B. Fine, "At Ease," *Beauty Biz*, February 2007, 31.

CHAPTER 6

p. 34: "The best ever, no doubt . . ." Quoted in Kieran O'Dwyer, "A Cutter Above," *Sporting News*, July 27, 2006, 24.

p. 35: "If it wasn't for him . . ." Quoted in Tom Pedulla, "Yankees' Rivera Has Finishing Touch," *USA Today*, October 25, 1999. http://www.usatoday.com/sports/baseball/99play/wsfs42.htm

p. 37: "Mariano's pitch is the best . . ." Quoted in Mel Antonen, "Yanks' Rivera Continues to Learn," *USA Today*, October 10, 2006. http://www.usatoday.com/sports/soac/2006-10-09-rivera_x.htm

CHAPTER 7

p. 40: "One day you are rich . . ." Quoted in Carol Sowers, "Teacher Creates Spanish Children's Magazine," *The Arizona Republic*, September 27, 2007.

p. 42: "My husband and I realized . . ." Quoted in Ximena Diego, "Spanish-Speaking Iguana Turns Three," *Criticas*, June 15, 2008. http://www.criticasmagazine.com/article/CA6560349.html

p. 43: "We thought it was a . . ." Quoted in René Colato Lainez, "An Interview with Christianne

Meneses Jacobs, Editor of Revista Iguana," *La Bloga*, August 22, 2007.

p. 43: "Our students are only taught. . ." Quoted in René Colato Lainez, "An Interview with Christianne Meneses Jacobs, Editor of Revista Iguana."

CHAPTER 8

p. 46: "My very first encounter with . . ." Quoted in Laurie Sandell, "Surprise! She's a Bombshell," *Glamour*, Vol. 105, Issue 10, p. 288.

p. 46: "I love to dance so . . ." Quoted in Jenny Comita, "Hot Betty," *W Magazine*, May 2007.

p. 49: "You just loved her because . . ." Quoted in Gustavo Arellano, "American Beauty," *Latina*, March 2007.

CROSS-CURRENTS

p. 50: "Three in four [Americans] have . . ." "Three in four . . ." "Immigration," Gallup, 2008. http://www.gallup.com/poll/1660/Immigration.aspx

p. 52: "I see the world from. . ." "Transcript: Life on the Border; Is Sealing the U.S.–Mexico Border Really Possible?" CNN, October 3, 2007. http://transcripts.cnn.com/TRANSCRIPTS/0710/03/oito.01.html

p. 52: "I grew up being . . ." Patricia Sheridan, "Carlos Mencia," *Pittsburgh Post-Gazette*, August 6, 2007.

p. 54: "We want to compete . . ." Sara Miller Llana and Amanda Paulson, *Christian Science Monitor*, June 13, 2006. http://www.csmonitor.com/2006/0613/p01s01-ussc.html

GLOSSARY

aeronautics—the science of flight.

alien—a foreign-born resident who has not become a naturalized citizen.

assimilate—to become part of a mainstream society or culture.

audition—a short, test performance by an actor applying for a role.

barrio—Spanish for district or neighborhood; a neighborhood in a U.S. city in which Spanish is commonly spoken.

colonize—to establish a colony, which is a region under the political control of another country's government.

earned run average (ERA)—a measure of a pitcher's efficiency; the number of earned runs allowed per nine innings.

emigrant—a person who moves away from his or her country to settle in another country or region.

Emmy—annual award given by the Academy of Television Arts and Sciences to recognize outstanding achievement in television.

ethnic—belonging to a particular group by descent or culture.

heritage—cultural practices and traditions that are passed down from one's ancestors; background.

iguana—large, plant-eating tropical lizard native to tropic regions of Central and South America and the Caribbean.

immigrant—a person who comes to live in a new country or region.

isthmus—a narrow strip of land connecting two larger areas of land. Central America is an isthmus connecting North America and South America.

Latin America—the parts of the Americas where the national language is Latin-based, especially Spanish and Portuguese. Latin America includes countries in South America and Central America, as well as the country of Mexico.

NASA—National Aeronautics and Space Administration; the government agency responsible for the exploration and study of space.

naturalized citizen—a person who has officially acquired the rights of nationality in a country after being born somewhere else.

poll—a survey, often conducted over the phone, in person, or over the Internet, in which the public's attitudes about specific issues are documented.

yoga—a Hindu discipline that aims to achieve a state of perfect spiritual insight and tranquility.

FURTHER READING

Christopher, Matt and Stout, Glenn. *The New York Yankees: Legendary Sports Teams*. New York: Little, Brown Young Readers, 2008.

Hunter, Miranda. *Latino Americans and Immigration Laws: Crossing the Border*. Broomall, Pa.: Mason Crest Publishers, 2005.

Levin, Judith. *Mariano Rivera*. New York: Chelsea House Publications, 2008.

Norwich, Grace. *America the Beautiful: An Unauthorized Biography*. New York: Price Stern Sloan, 2007.

Schwartz, Eric. *Central American Immigrants to the United States: Refugees from Unrest*. Broomall, Pa.: Mason Crest Publishers, 2005.

Spangenburg, Ray. *Onboard the Space Shuttle*. New York: Franklin Watts, 2002.

Turlington, Christy. *Living Yoga: Creating a Life Practice*. New York: Hyperion, 2002.

INTERNET RESOURCES

http://www.abc.go.com/primetime/uglybetty
The official Web site *Ugly Betty,* which is broadcast by the American Broadcasting Company television network. It includes cast biographies, episode recaps, photos, and full episodes that can be viewed online.

http://www.carlosmencia.com
The official Web site of comedian Carlos Mencia. It contains biographical information, tour information, and video clips of Carlos Mencia's performances.

http://www.christyturlington.com
The official Web site of former model and anti-smoking activist Christy Turlington Burns. The site contains a biography and information on various projects in which the former supermodel is currently involved.

http://www.gallup.com
The official Web site of the Gallup Organization, an international polling institute. It includes in-depth articles on issues and the results of polls taken by the organization.

http://www.migrationpolicy.org
An independent, nonpartisan, nonprofit think tank dedicated to the study of the movement of people worldwide. The site contains articles and fact sheets dealing with various facets of immigration.

http://www.nasa.gov
The official Web site of the National Aeronautics and Space Administration. The Web site includes articles and videos featuring past space missions and previews of those to come.

OTHER SUCCESSFUL AMERICANS OF CENTRAL AMERICAN HERITAGE

Maurice Benard (1963–): Daytime television actor born of Nicaraguan and Salvadoran parents. He has won a Daytime Emmy for his role on *General Hospital*, and has also been a regular on *All My Children*. In 1991 he portrayed Desi Arnaz in the made-for-television movie *Lucy & Desi: Before the Laughter*.

Rod Carew (1945–): Panamanian-born major league baseball player who was the American League Rookie of the Year in 1967. He won seven batting titles in his career and was elected to the National Baseball Hall of Fame in 1991.

Barbara Carrera (1951–): Nicaraguan-born television and film actress. She is famous for her role in the James Bond movie *Never Say Never Again*, for which she earned a Golden Globe nomination. She also had roles in the popular television series *Dallas* and the mini-series *Centennial*.

Rosie Casals (1948–): American tennis player born of Salvadoran parents. She won 12 Grand Slam doubles tournaments during her career and was elected to the International Tennis Hall of Fame in 1996.

Francisco Goldman (1954–): American-born novelist and journalist of Guatemalan descent. In 1992, his first novel—*The Long Night of White Chickens*—won the Sue Kaufman Prize for First Fiction awarded by the American Academy of Arts and Letters. After working for years as an investigative journalist, he wrote *The*

Art of Political Murder: Who Killed the Bishop. It is an account of the assassination of Guatemalan Bishop Juan José Gerardi Conedera.

Carmela Gloria Lacayo (1949–): President and CEO of the National Association for Hispanic Elderly. Of Nicaraguan descent, Lacayo

Former Minnesota Twins star Rod Carew salutes the crowd at the 2008 Major League Baseball All-Star Game, held in New York City.

has worked to improve conditions for the Hispanic and low-income elderly. She also oversees the National Hispanic Research Center and is cofounder of Hispanas Organized for Political Equality.

Hermann Mendez (1949–): Guatemalan-born doctor who was one of the first physicians to recognize pediatric AIDS. He has received awards from the U.S. Department of Health and Human Services and the Assistant Secretary of Health for his work in the fight against the disease.

Hugo Pérez (1963–): Salvadoran soccer star who played professionally for 14 years. He was a member of the U.S. team that competed at both the 1988 Summer Olympics and the 1994 FIFA World Cup. He was inducted into the National Soccer Hall of Fame in 2008.

Hilda Solis (1957–): The daughter of Mexican and Nicaraguan immigrants, Solis is the only member of Congress of Central American descent. She has represented California's 32nd Congressional District in the U.S. House of Representatives since 2001. In 2008 Solis was chosen by president-elect Barack Obama to serve in his cabinet as U.S. Secretary of Labor.

Madeleine Stowe (1958–): American actress of Costa Rican descent. Since the 1970s she has appeared on various television shows and in TV movies. She has also starred in numerous films, including *The Last of the Mohicans* (1992), *Twelve Monkeys* (1995), and *The General's Daughter* (1999). In 2005 she won an Imagen Foundation award for Best Actress—Television.

Born in a suburb of Los Angeles, actress Madeleine Stowe is of Costa Rican ancestry.

David Unger (1950–): Guatemalan-born author and translator. He is the author of *Neither Caterpillar Nor Butterfly* and *The Girl in the Treehouse*. In addition, he has translated the works of Roque Dalton, Marion Benedetti, Sergio Ramírez, Luisa Valenzuela and others. He was awarded the 1998 Ivri-Nasawi Poetry Prize.

INDEX

Photo captions are noted in *bold italic*.

Belize, 5, *8*
bilingual programs, 44, 54. *See also* English language
Blackman, Rolando
  awards and honors, 17, 18, 19, 22
  basketball career, 17, 18–22, 52
  birth and family, 17
  as a broadcaster and coach, *17*, 22
  community work, 22
  education, 18–19, 22
  immigration, 17–18
Bledel, Alexis, *48*

Campbell, Naomi, *30*, 31
Carew, Rod, 36, 54, 60
census. *See* U.S. Census Bureau
Central America, 6, 7–10. *See also* individual countries
Chang-Díaz, Franklin
  astronaut career, 14–15
  awards and honors, 16
  birth and family, 12
  education, 13–14
  immigration and citizenship, 13, 14
  inspiration for career, 12, 13, 14
  research career, 14, 16
  space missions, 15

civil wars, 9
Corrao, Lauren, 26
Costa Rica, 5, *8*, 12, 13
Crawford, Cindy, 30
CSI: Crime Scene Investigation, 47

Dallas Mavericks, 17, 22

earthquakes, 9
Eckersley, Dennis, 34
El Salvador, 5, *8*, 9, 10, 29, 33
English language, 10
Evangelista, Linda, 30

Ferrera, America
  acting career, 46–49
  awards and honors, *45*, 47, 49
  birth and family, 45–46
  education, 46, 47
  and Ryan Piers Williams, 47
  and Salma Hayek, 48
  Ugly Betty, 45
Ford, Eileen, 29

Gallup Organization, 8, 10–11, 16, 50, 51, 53, 59
Gotta Kick It Up, 46–47
Guatemala, 5, *8*, 9

Harris, Devin, *17*
Hayek, Salma, 48
Heron, Chico, 35–36
Hoffman, Trevor, 38
Homeland Security, 10

Honduras, 5, *8*, 9, 10, 23, 24, 45
hurricanes, 9
Hyltin, Sterling, *33*

Iguana, 39, 42–44
immigration. *See also* U.S. Census Bureau
  attitudes toward, 50, 52
  and the English language, 10–11
  factors affecting, 9–10
  illegal, 8
  to the U.S., 7–10, 40

Jacobs, Christianne Meneses, *42*
  awards and honors, *39*
  bilingual programs, 44, 54
  birth and family, 39–40
  education, 40–41
  marriage, 41
  publishing career, 42–44
  teaching career, 41
Jacobs, Marc, 41, 43, 54
John F. Kennedy Space Center, *14*, *51*
Jordan, Michael, 21

Klein, Calvin, 30

Latino
  actors and entertainers, 60, 61. *See also* Ferrera, America; Mencia, Carlos
  astronauts. *See* Chang-Díaz, Franklin

athletes, 60, 61. *See also* Blackman, Rolando; Rivera, Mariano

communities, 11

culture, 10, 41–42, 43, 44

humanitarians, 60, 61

models. *See* Turlington, Christy

portrayals, *23*. See also *Ugly Betty*

role models, 43, 49

scientists. *See* Chang-Díaz, Franklin

writers, 60, 61. *See also* Jacobs, Christianne Meneses

Lively, Blake, *48*

Living Yoga: Creating a Life Practice, 31

Los Angeles, 11, 24, *40*, 45

Macpherson, Elle, *30*, 31

Mathews, Eddie, 52

Mencia, Carlos
  awards and honors, *23*, 25, 26
  birth and family, 23–24
  comedy career, 24–27, 59
  and controversy, 26–27, 52
  education, 24
  immigration, 23–24
  marriage and children, 26
  and TV/film appearances, 26, 27

Mind of Mencia, 26

NASA, 14–16, 51, 59

New York Knicks, 20–22

New York Yankees, *34*, 35, 36–38

NicaGal, 44

Nicaragua, 5, *8*, 9, 10, 39–40, 41

Panama, 5, *8*, 17, 18, 34, 35, 36, 54

Patric, Jason, 31

Plainsong, 47

Raybourn, Herb, 36

Real Women Have Curves, 47

Riley, Pat, 22

Rivera, Mariano
  awards and records, 36, 37–38
  baseball career, 35, 36–38
  birth and family, 34–35
  childhood, 35
  marriage and children, *38*
  and other ball players, 34, 37, 38
  pitching arsenal, 36, 37

Sandinista government, 9, 39–40

Schiffer, Claudia, *30*, 31

Slater, Christian, 31

smoking bans, 32, 53

Sports Illustrated, 19, 52

Starks, John, 22

Take a Joke, America, 25

Tamblyn, Amber, *48*

television, primetime, 54

Temporary Protected Status (TPS), 10

The Heartbreak Kid, 27

The Sisterhood of the Traveling Pants movies, 47, 49

Thome, Jim, 37

Touched by an Angel, 47

Turlington, Christy
  as antismoking advocate, 32, 53, 59
  birth and family, 28, *31*
  and business ventures, 29, 30, 31
  and charity work, 32–33
  education, 29, 31
  marriage and children, 31, *33*
  modeling career, 28–30, 59
  and spiritual interests, 31, 59

Ugly Betty, *23*, 45, 48–49, 59. *See also* television, primetime

U.S. Census Bureau, 5, 7–8, 10

Williams, Ryan Piers, 47

Wilson, Roger, 31

Yankee Stadium, *34*

Yo Sé!, 44

PICTURE CREDITS

ABOUT THE AUTHOR

John F. Grabowski is a teacher and freelance writer from Staten Island, New York. His published work includes 50 books; a nationally syndicated sports column; and articles for newspapers, magazines, and programs of professional sports teams. He has also provided consultation on several math textbooks and sold comedy material to Jay Leno, Joan Rivers, Yakov Smirnoff, and numerous other comics.